Especially for

Terri

From

Aunt Joy

Date

07-M-2016

Grand Moments
for
Grandmothers

Tina Krause

BARBOUR
PUBLISHING

Written and compiled by Tina Krause.

ISBN 978-1-60260-817-7

Published by Barbour Publishing, Inc., P.O. Box 719, Uhrichsville, Ohio 44683, www.barbourbooks.com

Our mission is to publish and distribute inspirational products offering exceptional value and biblical encouragement to the masses.

Member of the
Evangelical Christian
Publishers Association

Printed in China.

Contents

INTRODUCTION

It's Grand to Be a Grandma!

The phone signals the good news. "Mom," your son says breathlessly, "the baby is here!" After phoning a few family members, you dash to the hospital to meet your first grandchild.

Your son, still in hospital garb, leads you to the bassinet where his son sleeps. It is love at first sight as you examine every tiny feature and soft crease. "Hello, little sweetie," you whisper. "I'm your grandma."

"When a child is born, so are grandmothers," reads one quote. Just as one day slips into another, a mother becomes a grandmother seemingly overnight. The new arrival launches a new beginning with years of adventures, joys, blessings, and laughter ahead.

Whether you are a first-time grandma, a seasoned one, or a grandma-in-waiting, this book is devoted to all the doting, loving, proud, and even silly grandmas who know from experience that it is grand to be a grandma!

SECTION 1
Grand Moments
of Love

The First Brush of God's Love

My maternal grandmother was a round, robust woman with busy hands, a gentle spirit, and a loving heart. Her devotion to God, her family, and her church stretched outward with tentacles of tenderness.

One warm summer's day when I was a young child, Grandma tucked me in her bed for a nap. Through the open window a cool breeze brushed across my face, dispelling the heat. Fully contented and secure, I pressed my cheek deeper into the fluffy pillow enveloped in grandmother's crisp, freshly ironed pillowcase. Meanwhile, I listened to Grandma hum softly as she kneaded bread dough in the kitchen just outside the bedroom door.

Long before I would ever hear or sing the words of the ageless hymn, "Blessed assurance, Jesus is mine, O what a foretaste of glory divine. . . ," I sensed God's love and assurance through my grandmother's peaceful, godly manner.

Grandmothers have the unique privilege to touch their grandchildren's lives in unseen ways like no one else can. They are affectionate avenues by which young grandchildren travel on their pathways toward God. Before a child will recognize the love of God, he or she will find Him in the loving presence of a grandma.

My grandmother passed away when I was only seven years old. Yet I still remember with fondness the gentle breeze of God's love that first brushed the face of my spirit through the hands and heart of my grandma.

The love of God is shed abroad in our hearts by the Holy Ghost which is given unto us.

ROMANS 5:5 KJV

*Perfect love sometimes
does not come until
the first grandchild.*

WELSH PROVERB

God's Love Carries Them

Dear Lord,
It's hard to believe that as much as I love my grandchild,
You love her more. I pray for You to keep Your hand upon
her life. Please protect her and keep her safe. And as
she grows, draw her nearer to You as You pour out Your
love in bountiful measures. May Your abiding love carry
her throughout her lifetime, just as Your love carries me.
Amen.

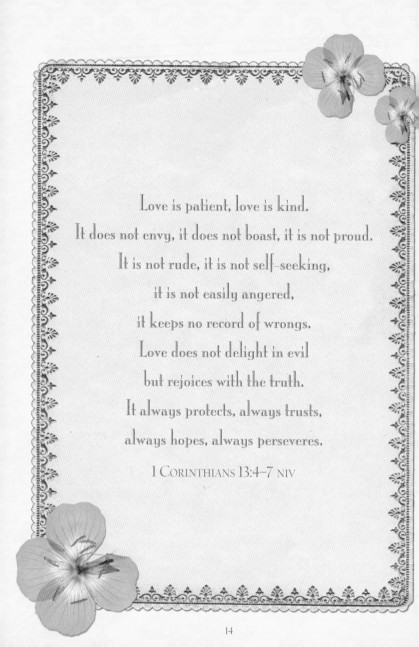

Love is patient, love is kind.

It does not envy, it does not boast, it is not proud.

It is not rude, it is not self-seeking,

it is not easily angered,

it keeps no record of wrongs.

Love does not delight in evil

but rejoices with the truth.

It always protects, always trusts,

always hopes, always perseveres.

1 CORINTHIANS 13:4–7 NIV

A Grandma's Unconditional Love

One of the grand characteristics of being a grandma is that we marinate in love for our grandchildren while viewing them through rose-colored bifocal glasses!

In fact, if one had to describe the character of grandmas, one need only read the "Love Chapter" of 1 Corinthians 13. The scriptures tell us that loving grandmas are patient and kind. They don't hold grudges when their grandkids do something wrong, and they are loyal to them no matter the cost. They always believe in their grandchildren, expect the best of them, and stand their ground in defending them.

Grandmothers possess an innate unconditional love when it comes to their offspring's offspring. In a grandmother's eyes, grandchildren are the best thing since ice cream and just as yummy. So it's easy to underscore our grandchildren's attributes and minimize their faults (they have so few anyway). With pride, we encourage and praise our grandchildren's individuality, and we support them unequivocally.

A grandmother's primary responsibility is to love, laugh, and enjoy the precious ones that have come into her life. What a grand role to embrace! After all, it is grandchildren who put the "grand" in grandma.

What children need most
are the essentials that
grandparents provide in abundance.
They give unconditional love,
kindness, patience, humor,
comfort, lessons in life.
And, most importantly, cookies.

RUDOLPH GIULIANI

Limitless Love

Dear Lord,

When I think of my grandchild, I think of Your love.
Your love knows no boundaries and stretches to our
inner core. You see us through the eyes of forgiveness
and grace, and You are long-suffering and merciful.
That's how I love my precious grandchild, Lord. Please
encompass him today and every day of his life. May he
forever know Your love and grace and never doubt that
love. . .not even for a moment.
Amen.

For God is not unrighteous to forget your work and labour of love, which ye have shewed toward his name.

<small>Hebrews 6:10 kjv</small>

SECTION 2
Grand Moments of Blessings

And he will love thee, and bless thee,
and multiply thee: he will also
bless the fruit of thy womb.

Deuteronomy 7:13 kjv

Blessings from the Heart of a Grandchild

The ailing grandmother was determined to muster the strength to get dressed to go to church on Sunday morning.

Her four-year-old grandson had not seen his grandma in quite some time due to her illness. As the boy and his parents entered the church sanctuary, he noticed his grandmother sitting in the pew. Delighted to see her, he raced to her arms, laughing and hugging her neck. And for the entire service, he nestled on her lap, resting his head on her shoulder.

Then midway through worship, he unexpectedly looked up and cupped his small hands around her chin. With a loving smile he said, "Grammy, you look so beautiful." Blessed beyond words, the sickly grandmother choked back her tears. She knew that no amount of makeup could conceal her infirmity, yet her grandson saw beyond her haggard face to admire the inner beauty of her soul.

Grandchildren are a blessing from the Lord like none other. They revive our youth and transform our spirits. On a rough day, a grandchild's hugs, sweet words, and cute expressions dilute our problems. And suddenly, nothing else matters.

The love of God is strikingly similar. No amount of sin diminishes what He feels for us. Rather, the Lord ignores our imperfections to expose the inner beauty of a life surrendered to Christ. Much like the love of a small boy for his grandmother, God blesses us with compassion and understanding as He embraces us with warm hugs and gentle smiles. And He often accomplishes that through the love of a grandchild.

Our grandchildren accept us for ourselves,

without rebuke or effort to change us,

as no one in our entire lives has ever done,

not our parents, siblings, spouses, friends—

and hardly ever our own grown children.

RUTH GOODE

Bless Him Back

Dear God,
If I were to search for a blessing, I would find a rich
abundance in the heart of my grandchild. I pray that
my life will bless him in even greater measures than he
already blesses me. Protect him from danger and harm
and keep him in the gentle palm of Your hand. Thank
You for Your love, and his. Pure. Simple. Genuine.
Amen.

A Name for Grandma

"I've always disliked the name Nana," one first-time grandmother protested. "Gran, Grandma, Grammy, even Nanny. . .anything but Nana!"

Then one day her daughter-in-law phoned to tell her, "Mom, little Alex named you today. . . . When he saw your photo, he called you Nana. I know you don't like that name, but. . ."

It was a sealed deal. The Precious One had spoken, and in one recognizable utterance, he named her Nana.

The following day, her daughter-in-law visited with eighteen-month-old Alex. From the back of the house, the grandmother heard tiny toddler feet pitter-patter through the living room as a sweet baby voice echoed, "Na-na, Na-na!"

In an instant, the grandmother ascended from Granny groveling to Nana nirvana. "Nana" was the prettiest, most honored name she had ever heard. "Nana is here," she swooned. "Yes, my love, your nana is here," she said as she swooped her grandbaby into her arms and smothered him with hugs and kisses.

One of the grandest blessings for a grandmother is to hear her grandchild say her name for the very first time. And not just any name. . .the name he or she gives her. What a grand moment to savor that special honor, knowing that somewhere in her grandchild's undeveloped speech and inquisitive mind, he or she found a name for grandma. . .the best name of all!

And I will make of thee a great nation,
and I will bless thee, and make thy name
great; and thou shalt be a blessing:
And I will bless them that bless thee.

GENESIS 12:2–3 KJV

*We should all have one person
who knows how to bless us
despite the evidence.
Grandmother was that person to me.*

PHYLLIS THEROUX

Blessings Appreciated

My heavenly Father,
The blessings You bestow are beyond what I deserve.
And often I miss their arrivals. But the arrivals of my
grandchildren are events I'll never forget. I praise You for
them and for what their lives have brought into my life.
Although I don't mention it nearly enough, I am grateful
for each and every gift. May I never take Your boundless
blessings for granted.
Amen.

Bless the LORD, O my soul: and all that is within me. . . . Bless the LORD, O my soul, and forget not all his benefits.

SECTION 3
Grand Proud Moments

Let another praise you,
and not your own mouth.

PROVERBS 27:2 NIV

Grandma's Bragging Rights

Grandmas hold bragging rights. . .it is part of their job description, topping the list with spoiling. When our children were small, we would never brag about them—at least not blatantly so—and we were intolerant of parents who did.

So why is it acceptable to brag about our grandchildren, but not our children? Maybe it's because having parented most of our lives, we've earned that grand grandparent honor.

Grandmothers are instinctively proud of their grandchildren. In fact, the role of grandma is probably the only one in which pride is an acceptable attribute. With admiration oozing from our pores, we boast about our grandchildren's talents and abilities. And should someone ask about our children's children, we flaunt our photo portfolios brimming with pictures.

"Our three-year-old Isaac is a budding musician," gushed one grandma. "He loves to sing and play instruments. With the ear of a maestro, he memorizes new songs in seconds. Music fills our SUV for him, while seven-year-old Ian sits in the far back seat reading books and retaining everything. Later, pen poised, he quizzes me on Bible, science, and historical trivia. And he usually wins. Remarkable! They're both so smart and talented!"

Although the scriptures frown upon singing self praises, the directive is inapplicable when boasting about our grandchildren. Grandmothers seem to know that intuitively. Grandchildren are a grandmother's crown and glory, so why not hold the high distinction of bragging about them?

By the way, did I tell you how exceptional my granddaughter is? She. . .

*No cowboy was ever faster on the draw
than a grandparent pulling
a baby picture out of a wallet.*

UNKNOWN

Unabashed Boasting

Dear Lord,
Your Word instructs us to refrain from bragging about
ourselves, but You give no clear direction on boasting
about our grandchildren. Everything about them makes
me so proud. Forgive me when I act and speak a tad
excessively, but thank You for the honor of unabashed
boasting!
Amen.

*"Let not the wise man boast of his wisdom
or the strong man boast of his strength
or the rich man boast of his riches, but let
him who boasts boast about this: that he
understands and knows me, that I am the
Lord, who exercises kindness...."*

Jeremiah 9:23–24 niv

Grandmothers Soothe, not Spoil

Parents often accuse grandmothers of spoiling their grandkids. "I don't spoil," one grandma stated flatly. "I soothe. There's a difference." Then with a certain smugness she added, "Besides, I understand her."

Long before a child utters her first words, a grandmother respects her grandchild's opinion. If a toddler spits green beans into her milk, she is experimenting with colors. When she blurts out, "No!" she is merely communicating a thought she is unable to fully express. If she scribbles crayon across the table, it is because her precocious gift of artistry outshines the limitations of an 8x10 sheet of paper. If a new toy loses her interest, it is due to the child's exceptional mental capabilities. And when she squirms in her car seat announcing, "I'm stuck!" a grandma declares her own seat-belt restriction replying, "I'm stuck, too!"

Proud grandmothers not only understand their grandchildren, their grandchildren understand them, too. Or as one woman—obviously a grandma—noted, "One is taught by experience to put a premium on those few people who can appreciate you for what you are." Those "few people" are our grandchildren. So who wouldn't spoil. . .rather, soothe. . . people like that?

I don't intentionally spoil my grandkids.
It's just that correcting them takes
more energy than I have left.

GENE PERRET

An Understanding Heart

Dear Jesus,
Thank You for the grand role of "Grandma" and all that
involves. I am so grateful to invest my life into the life
of this child. I ask for an understanding ear with which
to listen and a kind voice with which to share and pray.
Whether he is five or fifteen, I pray I will be available to
love and understand my grandchild whenever he needs
me most.
Amen.

*But from everlasting to everlasting the
Lord's love is with those who fear him,
and his righteousness
with their children's children.*

Psalm 103:17 niv

SECTION 4
Grand Faith—
Legacy Moments

A God-fluential Grandma

The significance of a grandmother's faith and influence on her grandchild is evident throughout the scriptures. The most notable example is recorded in the New Testament.

Timothy was a young preacher whose mother, Eunice, and grandmother, Lois, raised him in a Christian home. Bible scholars maintain that his grandmother was the first in his family to convert to Christianity. After doing so, she shared Christ with her daughter, Eunice, and together the mother and grandmother raised Timothy in the ways of the Lord.

In his letter to Timothy, the apostle Paul expressed joy that his coworker and "spiritual son" inherited the same genuine and heartfelt faith of his godly grandmother and mother.

Grandmothers have the special privilege of leaving behind the most valuable inheritance—namely, a living legacy of unfeigned faith. Women who live for Christ and share their Christian lifestyle with their grandchildren will influence them for the kingdom of God. As a grandchild witnesses a grandmother's consecration to God and answered prayers, his or her faith grows.

One quotation says, "The humblest individual exerts some influence, either for good or evil, upon others" (Henry Ward Beecher). We need not possess wealth or lofty accomplishments in order to make a difference in a child's life. We need only to live for God and teach our grandchildren to do the same. Because in the grand scheme of things, our grandest achievements are our grandchildren.

When I call to remembrance
the unfeigned faith that is in thee,
which dwelt first in thy grandmother Lois,
and thy mother Eunice;
and I am persuaded that in thee also...

2 Timothy 1:5 kjv

A hundred years from now it will not matter
what my bank account was, the sort of house
I lived in, or the kind of car I drove. . .
but the world may be different because
I was important in the life of a child.

FOREST E. WITCRAFT

A Legacy of Unfeigned Faith

Lord,
I once thought that my days of making a difference were past. As a grandma, I know better. Lord, help me to influence my grandchildren for Your kingdom. Create in me an example of Christian faith that will ultimately guide them to the cross of Christ. Just as Timothy became a man of God due to the godly influence of his mother and grandmother, help me to be a living legacy of unfeigned faith for my grandchildren.
Amen.

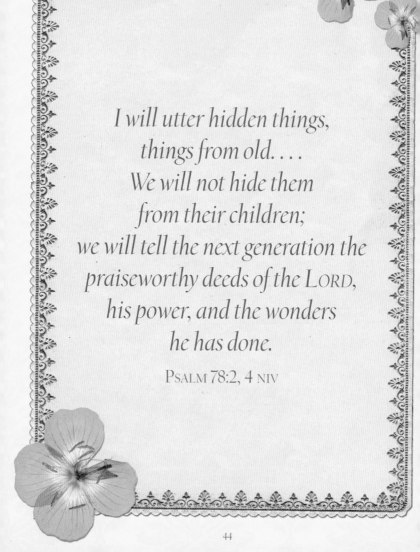

I will utter hidden things,
things from old. . . .
We will not hide them
from their children;
we will tell the next generation the
praiseworthy deeds of the LORD,
his power, and the wonders
he has done.

PSALM 78:2, 4 NIV

Grandma's Voice

"Nana." Ian nudged his grandma. "Tell me a story about. . .um, um. . .Little Bear getting cold!"

Grandmothers are storytellers with the voices of many characters: Squeaky the Mouse, Peter Cottontail, Little Bear, and every other animal a child imagines. So grandmothers are known to weave stories on a whim. In modern-day parables, they share generational narrations of how God protects, empowers, and speaks to them.

"Once upon a time there lived Little Bear, Father Bear, and Mother Bear," she recites. Deepening her voice she continues. " 'Little Bear, it's time to fish for dinner,' said Father Bear, 'but before we go, we must pray for safety because it's cold out there and I see a big storm brewing.' "

Grandma's voice teaches a child to listen for God's voice. Yet the most lasting impressions come through personal example. Aside from parents, grandparents are the primary "voices" that grandchildren hear through imaginary play and verbal and nonverbal communication.

One of the grand pleasures of being a grandma is to use story moments to influence our grandchildren with the message of God's protection and love.

"Little Bear, do you hear that?"
    "Hear what, Nana Bear?"
"Do you hear God's love in the voice of your nana?"

I sure hope so. . .because it's cold out there, and who knows when the next storm will brew.

Grandchildren are the dots that connect the lines from generation to generation.

LOIS WYSE

Reflect Childlike Faith

Dear Lord,
Today I am watching a little one who is watching me,
too. I pray that my words and actions will reflect Your
love. Help me to trust You with childlike faith, just as
my grandchild trusts. May I emulate her simple faith
and heartfelt innocence. As I stand with my hands
outstretched toward heaven in prayer, may the tiny hands
I hold learn to praise You, too.
Amen.

*A good [woman] leaves an inheritance
for [her] children's children.*

PROVERBS 13:22 NIV

SECTION 5
Grand Moments of Discovery

*"Therefore, whoever humbles himself
like this child is the greatest
in the kingdom of heaven.
And whoever welcomes a little child
like this in my name welcomes me."*

MATTHEW 18:4–5 NIV

What a Discovery. . .
Every Room Occupied

After her granddaughter was born, a new grandma emptied one of her dresser drawers to fill with Baby's items. This is the place, she reasoned, that would house new toys and picture books for her granddaughter to explore each time she came to visit.

Twenty months later "Baby's drawer" evolved into "Baby's house." Evidence of her granddaughter is everywhere from tiny smudge prints where the little princess pressed her nose against the window, to a whole section of toys piled high in a spare bedroom. Her grandbaby's dresses hang in the closet, and a small dresser is jammed with everything from blankets to bibs. The TV room hosts a crib, and kids' DVDs stand like soldiers side by side. Even the kitchen cabinets harbor a shelf of sippy cups and character bowls.

This grandma, like so many other grandmothers before her, discovered that when our grandchildren enter this world they also enter our hearts. From then on, every part of our lives is touched by their coming.

A similar phenomenon occurs when we accept Christ. Suddenly, we yearn to spend time with Him and desire to know more about Him. We read God's Word to grow in knowledge and wisdom. And as we surrender every room of our spiritual homes to Him, He abides in every area of our lives.

Our love for our grandchildren impels us to open every nook and cranny of our home and hearts to them. Our love for God does the same. For our lives are forever touched by His coming. What an amazing discovery.

If your baby is "beautiful and perfect, never cries or fusses,
sleeps on schedule and burps on demand,
an angel all the time"; you're the grandma.

TERESA BLOOMINGDALE

Growth in Discoveries

Dear Lord,
Moments with my grandchild are moments of discovery.
Hand in hand, we explore birds in flight and analyze an
army of ants through a magnifying glass. Grand moments
with her remind me of my precious moments with You.
Jesus, keep me close at Your side. . .Your hand clasped in
mine, so that I might learn and continue to grow as You
unfold the discoveries of Your Word.
Amen.

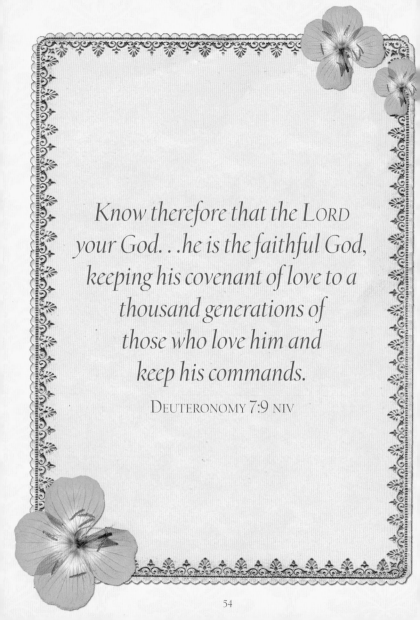

Know therefore that the LORD *your God. . .he is the faithful God, keeping his covenant of love to a thousand generations of those who love him and keep his commands.*

DEUTERONOMY 7:9 NIV

Discover New Eyes

"What's happened to you?" a husband asked his wife, a first-time grandma. Before her grandchild arrived, she whisked through malls in search of selfish finds. Now, she enters a store and dashes to the baby department to scan racks of baby clothes. She searches garage sales for used high chairs and play yards "just to have around" for her new grandbaby.

Just as everything changed when she became a mom, more changes occur as she transitions from Mom to Grandmother. For both grandma and grandchild, all of life and creation is a series of discoveries, a sequence of firsts. Her new grandbaby cries and her heart cries with him; he smiles and her heart dances. The first time he coos, takes a step, or reaches for her to pick him up is a milestone to record.

"The real voyage of discovery consists not in seeking new landscapes but in having new eyes," notes Marcel Proust. Children have new eyes. They marvel at a leaf plucked from a tree and curiously inspect a solitary blade of grass. They trust without question, embrace unconditionally, and learn faster than birds jetting skyward. With boundless inquisitiveness, they touch and absorb everything around them. A child's new eyes search for hidden discoveries, and they delight over the smallest conquests. And with them, so do grandmas.

So what happened to Grandma? New eyes. She acquired new eyes. And the view is incredible.

It's such a grand thing to be a mother
of a mother—that's why the world
calls her grandmother.

UNKNOWN

Praise for New Eyes

Dear Lord,
For me, the greatest day of discovery was when I first
embraced Your forgiveness and love. As a mom, I learned
more of what that means. Now, I thank You for changing
my life once again as I view all of life and creation through
the eyes of my grandchild. May my "new eyes" never dim,
even when my vision does!
Amen.

She speaks with wisdom, and faithful instruction is on her tongue.

PROVERBS 31:26 NIV

SECTION 6
Grand Second-Chance Moments

A Chance to Dote

The grandmother sat on the patio, sipping bottled water with her daughter and grandchildren. Noticing the dry bird bath, the two little girls began to pour the store-bought water into the stone vessel to fill it.

"Don't use the bottled water," their mom chided, "you're wasting it!"

With her eyes warmly transfixed on her grandchildren's play, the doting grandma replied, "Oh, let them; it's okay. There's plenty more where that came from."

Unlike when we were moms, grandmothers rarely grimace. What made us cringe as a mother makes us giggle as a grandmother. What was once a no-no is entertaining to us the second time around. We disdain discipline but love to boast about our grandchild's attributes and talents. It's as if God changes our very nature the instant we become a grandmother.

Perhaps it is because grandmas have walked the challenging road of motherhood years before. Along the way, we learned what issues to address and what to let go; what needs to be done, and what can wait. Regardless, all of life is viewed from a slower, gentler perspective now.

Similarly, God's character is a combination of loving parent and tender grandparent. Sometimes God administers parental discipline and direction. Most times, He applauds our smallest accomplishments, underscores our talents, and encourages our childlike faith.

And when we reach for an outpouring of His living water, just as the doting grandmother, He must muse, saying, "That's okay. There's plenty more where that came from."

And a little child shall lead them.

ISAIAH 11:6 KJV

Becoming a grandparent
is a second chance. . .it's all love
and no discipline.
There's no thorn in this rose.

DR. JOYCE BROTHERS

Thanksgiving for Second Chances

Dear Lord,
You are a God of second chances, and I'm so grateful for that. Thank You for the chance to right the wrongs I made the first time around.

As a grandma, help me to put to use all the good things that I learned as a mom and leave the not-so-good beneath Your forgiving grace.
Amen.

Roses without Thorns

Psychologist Dr. Joyce Brothers noted that being a grandmother is all love and little or no discipline. "There's no thorn in this rose," she wrote.

Although grandmothers *reluctantly* correct their grandchildren when needed, their expertise lies in their ability to delight in and enjoy the intuitive, creative, inquisitive things their grandchildren do and say.

Grandmas allow bubble-blowing in the bathtub, rather than isolating the messy mixture to outdoors. As the bubbles—especially the big ones—pop against the bathroom walls, they erupt with oohs and aahs in peals of laughter.

A trip to the toy store becomes an invitation to play with doll houses and dump trucks. Unrestrained, grandmas call attention to favorite toys and say, "Isn't this neat? Would you like one of these?" Ah yes, the thornless rose.

The scene was quite different when she was a young mom. Before entering a store with *her* children, she spouted lectures a college professor would envy. "Okay now, remember. . .*no* toys. We're looking for a birthday gift. So behave, or. . ." Ouch, a thorn.

Grandchildren are the roses in a grandmother's garden. And this time around, the roses have no thorns. How grand!

And the desert shall rejoice,
and blossom as the rose.

Isaiah 35:1 kjv

Moments to Savor

Dear God,
Every moment I spend with my grandchild is one birthed in heaven. With him, I stroll instead of taking giant strides, and I savor the smallest things. Through this child I recognize and acknowledge the beauty I once took for granted. Now I marvel at the blessings each day brings. . .each moment brings. Thank You, Jesus, for them all.
Amen.

A grandmother is a mother who has a second chance.

Unknown

But Jesus said,
Suffer little children,
and forbid them not, to come unto me:
for of such is the kingdom of heaven.

MATTHEW 19:14 KJV

SECTION 7
Grand Moments
of Joy

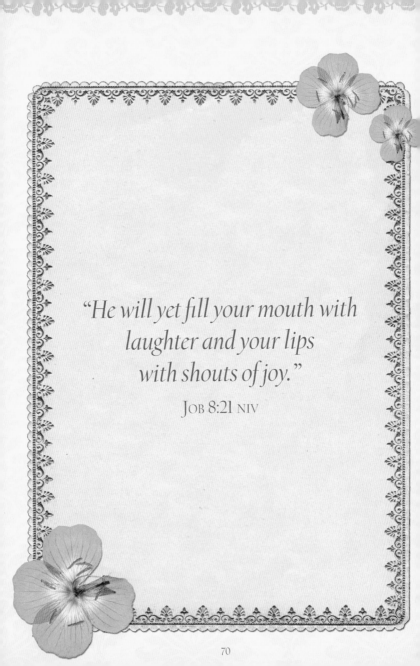

"*He will yet fill your mouth with laughter and your lips with shouts of joy.*"

JOB 8:21 NIV

Grandma's Joy

One early morning, three-year-old Kaitlyn stared at the face of her grandmother. As her grandma blinked open her eyes, Kaitlyn smiled and asked in a sweet, quiet voice, "Are you happy, Grandma?"

The groggy grandmother dismissed the fact that she had catnapped all night because her granddaughter—stretched across the width of the bed—left her teetering on the edge of the mattress. Instead, the blurry-eyed grandma whispered, "Oh yes, my precious girl. I'm happy whenever I'm with you. You give me lots of joy!"

Grandchildren are a grandmother's greatest joy. No wonder. From the moment they come into our lives, their priceless presence fills our homes and lives with happiness, wonderment, and a renewed zest for life.

With new excitement, grandmothers globe-trot to the zoo, the park, and the beach as they wrap themselves in the world of their grandchild. In joyful abandon, they run through sprinklers, create a Picasso from sand, and compose songs to the *clang* of kitchen utensils. With grandchildren they smile, dance, and laugh deep belly laughs.

God uses grandchildren in their innocence and simplicity to create fun moments of lasting joy. Through them, grandmothers play again.

When life overwhelms us with cell phones and busy schedules, and our problems stack higher than a pile of recyclable newspapers, the Lord gifts us with grandchildren to lighten the load and add joy and laughter just when we need it. Even after a sleepless night.

Cherish all your happy moments:
they make a fine cushion for old age.

BOOTH TARKINGTON

God Gives the Joy

Heavenly Father,
I hardly remember what it was like before my
granddaughter's smile brightened gloomy and difficult
days. With her, I emerge from the doldrums to happy
chatter, vibrant laughter, and warm hugs. Lord, as I focus
on this child, help me to always remember the One who
gave her to me. Thank You for Your joy. . .and mine.
Amen.

Recognizable Glowing Grandmas

It's easy to spot a grandma. She's the lady who beams each time her grandchild comes in view. Shrines of photographs garnish her walls, desk, and tabletops, while magnets secure her budding artist's artwork to the refrigerator door. When her granddaughter comes to visit, Grandma waits for her arrival on the front porch. And as her little princess leaves, she waves good-bye, shouting, "See ya later, alligator!" To which her grandchild responds, "After a while, crocodile!"

A grandma stops whatever she's doing to play, talk, or read to her little one. She keeps track of her grandchildren's growth spurts, jotting his heights on the wall behind a bedroom door. And with great resolve she states that if she should ever move, the piece of drywall—with all of the markings—will go with her.

Giving to her grandchildren is a pleasure, not a chore. A grandmother cooks made-to-order breakfasts and allows her grandchildren to stay up way past their bedtimes. On a whim, she embarks on adventures, taking her grandchildren wherever they want to go. And at all times she stocks her kitchen pantry and refrigerator with her grandchildren's favorite foods "just in case" they stop by.

Yes, grandmothers are easily recognizable. They are the grannies who glow with joy.

For what is our hope, our joy,
or the crown in which we will
glory in the presence of our
Lord Jesus when he comes?
Is it not you?
Indeed, you are our glory and joy.

1 Thessalonians 2:19–20 NIV

Grandmas don't just say "that's nice"—they reel back, roll their eyes, and throw up their hands and smile. You get your money's worth out of grandmas.

UNKNOWN

Bless This Joy

Dear Lord,

Thank You for each moment to enjoy my "little joy."
Give me the strength to invest all that I have and all that
I am into this gift I call my grandchild. I am grateful for
the gladness and love he brings me each time we are
together. Please return a double dose of happiness and
joy to him, I pray.
Amen.

*A cheerful look brings joy to the heart,
and good news gives health to the bones.*

PROVERBS 15:30 NIV

SECTION 8
Grand Moments of Time

To every thing there is a season,
and a time to every purpose
under the heaven.

ECCLESIASTES 3:1 KJV

Time and Seasons

Life, like the seasons, constantly changes. The springtime of a grandma's life was once filled with baby bottles, smudged faces, and bruised knees. Her social calendar consisted of unexpected pediatrician visits, school programs, and exhausting field trips. Endless motherly demands made her wonder if life would ever slow down.

Then the breathless heat of summer arrived with more changes as high school and college entered the landscape. Soon, her children married and had children of their own, as the cycle of life returned to the two people who started the whole process many seasons before. Only now, she reflects on how fast time has slipped past.

Seasons. They're all different, all necessary in the cycle of life; yet each season provides new lessons. The hustle and bustle of motherhood transitions to a season of grace as we pleasantly spend time enjoying grandmother moments. We inhale the refreshing breaths of springtime again through the giggles and playfulness of our grandchildren. But this time around, our lives are absent of parental demands—just pure pleasure with lots of time to spare.

The Bible notes that there is a time and a season to everything. . .a time to weep, a time to laugh, a time to plant, a time to reap, a time to mourn, a time to dance. . . (Ecclesiastes 3:1–8). As we enter the autumn of our lives, God desires for us to savor each moment we spend with our grandchildren. For in this season, it's time to dance!

The butterfly counts not months,
but moments, and has time enough.

RABINDRANATH TAGORE

Time Well Spent

Lord,
Time flies so quickly. Help me to take full advantage of each moment with my curious little one. Whether we gather fistfuls of dandelions or build forts with cushions and blankets, may I bask in the pure pleasure of time well spent.
Amen.

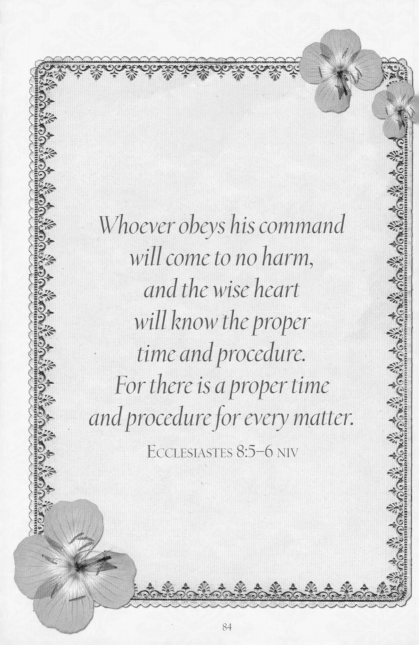

Whoever obeys his command
will come to no harm,
and the wise heart
will know the proper
time and procedure.
For there is a proper time
and procedure for every matter.

ECCLESIASTES 8:5–6 NIV

The Gift of Time

Grandmothers have time. And when they don't have it, they make it for their grandchildren. At a moment's notice, they stop whatever the task to devote unmitigated amounts of time to their grandchildren. And they do so cheerfully and willingly.

A grandma listens to her grandchildren's requests and tries hard to fulfill every one of them. She plays board games for hours, acting as if there's nothing else she would rather do. Before she cuddles up to watch videos with her grandchild on a chilly winter night, she first takes time to warm a blanket in the dryer to cover him. Lovingly, she serves a tray of cookies and hot chocolate with lots of marshmallows.

In a world full of no-no's, grandmothers seemingly offer an automatic "yes" to whatever her grandchild asks to do. Yes to baking cookies; yes to playing at the park; yes to exploring; yes to toy stores and ice cream shops; yes to lying on the ground to name animals made of clouds in the sky; yes to reading the same story over and over again.

Time is the gift grandmothers give effortlessly, immeasurably, and pleasurably. Time is a grand thing for grandmas. . .and grandchildren.

My name is No-no,
but my grandma calls me Precious.

UNKNOWN

Treasure Times of Pleasure

Dear God,
I treasure my time with my grandchildren. Our moments together are never wasted. We do important things like play dress-up with my high heels and costume jewelry, or we walk to the store to buy a snow cone after we play baseball. These are special times to remember. And by the way, Lord, thanks for butterflies. They give my grandchildren (and me) such pleasure.
Amen.

Children's children are a crown to the aged.

PROVERBS 17:6 NIV

SECTION 9
*Grand Moments
of Prayer*

A Grandmother's Powerful Prayers

"Mom," the son confessed, "Jamie is pregnant and we're going to get married." This was not the way the mother envisioned becoming a grandmother. She raised her son in a Christian home, but he had strayed.

Later that night, she fell to her knees in prayer. "O God," she pleaded, "please turn this bad situation around for good. Show me how to pray." In that moment, she committed to not only pray and fast one day each week for her son and his girlfriend, but for her unborn grandchild.

It was an arduous road to witness the worldly, sinful ways of her son and his new bride as they shared her home for four months after their baby was born. But she was steadfast. She covered her grandchild in constant prayer, singing him to sleep with old hymns like "Amazing Grace" and "There's Power in the Blood," fully trusting that God would bring the child's parents to the cross of Christ.

One day, the Lord spoke to the grandmother's heart saying, *"The best way you can love this child is to love his parents unconditionally."* With God's help she did, and soon her son and daughter-in-law prayed to accept Christ. Today, her grandson has two Christian parents, fully dedicated to the Lord. All because of a grandmother's prayers.

Grandmothers have the special privilege and responsibility to pray for their grandchildren. When they do, God answers in amazing ways. Do you carry a burden for your grandchild or adult child? Commit to pray. God is listening.

For this reason, since the day we heard
about you, we have not stopped praying
for you and asking God to fill you with the
knowledge of his will through all spiritual
wisdom and understanding.

COLOSSIANS 1:9 NIV

Grandmother—a wonderful mother with lots of practice.

<small>UNKNOWN</small>

A Whisper Away

Dear Lord,

Thank You for the privilege of prayer. When my family faces challenges and difficult circumstances, You are there. When my grandchildren need Your guidance, comfort, or protection, You are there. When I need Your assurance and peace, You are there. I am so grateful that You are only a whisper away. Thank You for always being there.

Amen.

I thank my God every time I remember you.
In all my prayers for all of you,
I always pray with joy.

PHILIPPIANS 1:3–4 NIV

Pass Down a Prayer Legacy

A framed print depicts a father kneeling at the bedside of his sleeping child. With head bowed the father prays, placing his hand on the boy's side. In the background, the starry night reflects what takes place in the spirit world when parents or grandparents intercede on behalf of their children or grandchildren. With uplifted arms, a mighty angel guards the home, pushing back the forces of evil that attempt to enter.

Intercessory prayer summons the power of the Holy Spirit and God's angelic armies to fight our spiritual battles and those of our grandchildren. Christian grandmothers understand that kind of prayer. After all, we have spent most of our adult lives praying for our children and now, our grandchildren.

How grand it is to pass down a prayer legacy from one generation to another. . .to know that one day our grandchildren's prayers will outdistance ours. Meanwhile, we not only pray *for* our grandchildren, we pray *with* them. In doing so, we teach them to depend on God and to talk to Him about anything, anywhere.

If we could view the spiritual realm, we would realize the potency and power of steadfast prayer. Despite what it may appear in the earthly realm, when we pray, God fights our battles. And He always wins.

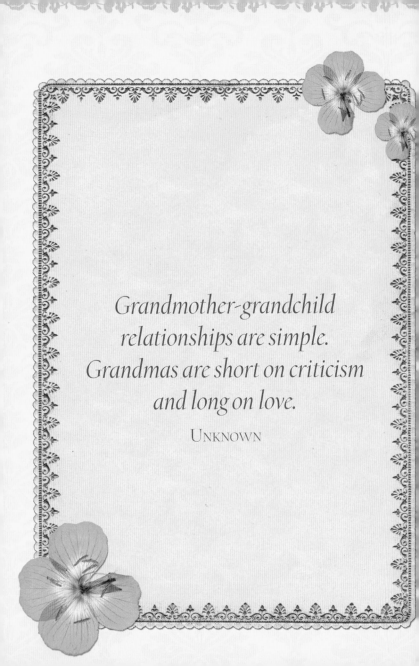

*Grandmother-grandchild
relationships are simple.
Grandmas are short on criticism
and long on love.*

Unknown